How We Know Jesus Is God?

Ralph O. Muncaster

HARVEST HOUSE PUBLISHERS
Eugene, Oregon 97402

Cover by Terry Dugan Design, Minneapolis, Minnesota

By Ralph O. Muncaster

Are There Hidden Codes in the Bible?

Can You Trust the Bible?

Creation vs. Evolution

Creation vs. Evolution Video

How Do We Know Jesus Is God?

Is the Bible Really a Message from God?

What Is the Proof for the Resurrection?

HOW DO WE KNOW JESUS IS GOD?
Copyright © 2000 by Ralph O. Muncaster
Published by Harvest House Publishers
Eugene, Oregon 97402

Library of Congress Cataloging-in-Publication Data

Muncaster, Ralph O.
    How Do We Know Jesus Is God? / Ralph O. Muncaster.
        p. cm. — (Examine the evidence series)
    Includes bibliographical references.
    ISBN 0-7369-0321-6
        1. Jesus Christ—Divinity. I. Title.

BT216 .M86 2000
232'.8—dc21   99-053618

00 01 02 03 04 05 06 07 08 09 / BP/ 10 9 8 7 6 5 4 3 2 1

Contents

Why Jesus?

Stop and Think

No person or group can come close to the vast impact of Jesus of Nazareth on the world. Even people who don't believe His claim to be God in human flesh do not deny His profound influence. Human morality, the world legal systems, the evolution of nations, and every date in history use His time on earth as a reference. Add to this the fact that about one-third of the world's population claims to be "Christian" with a billion people today directly affected by the teaching of Jesus.

The magnitude of such impact alone is reason for wondering if, in fact, God was involved in Jesus' time on earth.

Suppose the claims of billions of Christians and centuries of investigation are true. Suppose there is eternal life. Suppose the only way to know one can achieve it is through a relationship with Jesus. Suppose God is trying to reach each of us here on earth to help us improve everyday living? If such claims are true, then determining the role of Jesus is without a doubt the most important issue for one to understand in one's lifetime. More important than the next vacation, more important than the next golf game, and even more important than the next paycheck. It's incredible that any single person wouldn't take the time to at least "check it out."

Fortunately God has provided more evidence of Jesus and His role than of any other event in human history. We don't need to accept it on blind faith. Even so, like acceptance of any historical fact or religious belief, the ultimate decision to follow Jesus requires a final step of faith.

The Issues

Jesus Christ has been analyzed *far* more than anyone else in the history of the world.

1. To doubt the existence of Jesus is to doubt the reason for the largest movement in history. The deaths of early Christian martyrs who had been alive at the time of Jesus are undeniable. (see pp. 10–13)

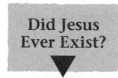

Did Jesus Ever Exist?

2. The existence of thousands of early manuscripts that survived eradication attempts provides greater credibility than virtually any other accepted historical fact. Some were written while eyewitnesses were still alive and withstood scrutiny by critics at the time. (see pp. 10–13)

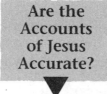

Are the Accounts of Jesus Accurate?

3. Even the staunchest enemies of Jesus acknowledged His miracles—recorded by the Jews and others at the time and available as evidence today. Did any non-Christians witness the resurrection? We don't know. Is it likely anyone would witness the resurrection yet not believe? And the evidence of those who *certainly* knew the truth is compelling. (see pp. 16–22)

Did the Miracles and Resurrection Really Occur?

4. Was Jesus really conceived of the Holy Spirit? Was He really God? Analysis of His claims and the perfect fulfillment of ancient prophecies provide very strong evidence of divine planning. (see pp. 24–29)

Do We Know That Jesus Was Sent by God? ▼

5. If Jesus was who He said He was—the incarnation of the God of truth—then His stated purpose must be true. He came not to condemn the world but to save it—a gift that gives joy in this world and a promise of eternal paradise. (see pp. 30–31)

What Was the Purpose of His Coming? ▼

6. The free gifts of peace on earth and eternity in heaven are available to all who believe in Jesus, ask forgiveness for their sins, and accept Jesus as Lord and director of their life. (see pp. 46–47)

What Should We Do As a Result?

Fortunately for us, evidence exists to examine these issues.

Historical Setting

The stage was perfectly set for the coming of Jesus of Nazareth.

The World Situation

Political Stability—Never before or since has such a large percentage of the world lived at peace under a single government. The Roman Empire had expanded to include much of Europe, Africa, and Asia. About half of the world's 138 million people were governed by Rome. And the peace known as *Pax Romana*, admired throughout history, lasted 200 years.

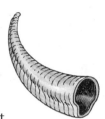

In 44 B.C. Julius Caesar was assassinated, and his throne went to his great-grandnephew, Octavian, who was given the title Caesar Augustus. After defeating Mark Antony and Cleopatra, Augustus ruled from 27 B.C. to A.D. 14. Augustus began the great peace reforms and ordered the worldwide census which caused Joseph and Mary to travel to Bethlehem at the time of Jesus' birth (Luke 2:1).

Transportation—For the first time in history, an elaborate network of highways and sea routes throughout the empire made transportation relatively easy. This was vital to the rapid spread of Christianity.

Communication—The world was becoming unified as the level of education increased and the language of Koine Greek (the dialect of the New Testament) was becoming common. As a result, it was easier and quicker to spread new ideas and thinking across a multicultural world than ever before.

Bethlehem, Nazareth, and Jerusalem

Jerusalem was the most prominent city in the Middle East. Along with being the political and religious center for the Jewish people, it was a regional seat of government for Rome and was the residence of Herod.

Nazareth was on a major trade route from the ports of Tyre and Sidon, known for both vice and prostitution—as was Nazareth. The great city of Sepphoris, just 4 miles from Nazareth, was the capital of Galilee in Jesus' youth and was being rapidly expanded to honor its new leader, Herod Antipas. As carpenters, Joseph and Jesus almost certainly spent time there. (Excavation of Sepphoris is far from complete.)

Bethlehem of Judea was a small rural town a few miles south of Jerusalem. Even in Jesus' day, Bethlehem had significance as the burial place of Rachel (Jacob's wife), the place of courtship of Ruth and Boaz, and the birthplace of King David.

Did Jesus Exist?

Virtually all major religions—even those opposing Him—acknowledge the existence of Jesus. For hundreds of years Jesus' existence was as widely accepted as Abraham Lincoln's existence is today. Only in relatively recent history have some people challenged it. Possibly in a few thousand years, Mr. Lincoln's existence may be challenged as well.

Christian Historical Records

The magnitude of the Christian record of Jesus stands far above any record of anyone who has ever lived upon this planet. Existing early manuscripts exceed 24,000. The earliest were written within 25 years of Jesus' death.[1] No work of antiquity approaches the Bible's documentary credibility, including *all* works we accept as historical fact. Some examples are:

Major Existing Manuscripts[1]	Early Records	From Event to First Existing Manuscript
Gallic Wars—Julius Caesar	10	1000 years
History—Pliny the Younger	7	750 years
History—Thucydides	8	1300 years
History—Herodotus	8	1300 years
Iliad—Homer *(Second most prevalent writing)*	643	500 years
The New Testament	**24,000+**	**25 years**

The vastness of the number of accounts of the resurrection is particularly extraordinary considering that:

1. *Jesus was not in a position of public importance.* He was not a king, not a religious leader, and not a general. Relative to Rome, Jesus came from a small, distant town and was a lowly carpenter with a scant three-year ministry. *Rome hardly knew of Him* until testimony of eyewitnesses later threatened political and religious stability.

2. *The records survived the most intensive eradication effort of all time.* Rapidly growing in number, Christian witnesses were killed, written records were burned, and anyone professing belief in Christ was executed. In A.D. 303 an edict was issued to destroy all of the world's Bibles. People found with Bibles were killed.

3. *There was no printing press, and the world population was low.* The number of surviving early manuscripts is absolutely staggering considering they were all *hand-copied* by a far smaller population base. Only 138 million people existed at the time, with no automatic duplication methods for the printed word. What motivated such extensive work?

Was the incredible *survival* of the Christian record a miracle or just the senseless expansion of a myth? Why haven't other religions—with more prominent leaders, with lifelong ministries, and with less persecution—produced similar evidence? *Something major happened.*

Non-Christian Evidence

Very few written works *of anything* exist from the period of A.D. 30 to A.D. 60. All works from A.D. 50 to A.D. 60 are said to fit in bookends only a foot apart.[1] In the years after Nero's killing of Christians in A.D. 64 we find the following references to Jesus and His followers:

Thallus (circa A.D. 52)—Historical work referenced by Julius Africanus explains the darkness at the time of Christ's death as a solar eclipse. While an eclipse did not occur in that period (pointed out by Julius Africanus), a reference to Jesus' death is presented as fact.

Josephus (circa A.D. 64–93)—This Jewish historian referenced Jesus, His miracles, His crucifixion, and His disciples. Also referenced are James " . . . brother of Jesus who was called the Christ," and John the Baptist.

Cornelius Tacitus (A.D. 64–116)—Writing to dispel rumors that Nero caused the great fire of Rome in A.D. 64, he refers to Christians as the followers of "Christus," who "had undergone the death penalty in the reign of Tiberius, by sentence of the procurator Pontius Pilatus." The resurrection was called "the pernicious superstition."

Pliny the Younger (circa A.D. 112)—As governor of Bithynia (Asia Minor), he requested guidance from Rome regarding the proper test to give Christians before executing them. (If they renounced the faith, cursed Jesus and worshiped the statue of the emperor Trajan, they were set free.)

Hadrian (circa A.D. 117–138)—In response to questions regarding the punishment of Christians who drew people away from pagan gods, which affected the sale of idols, Hadrian commanded that

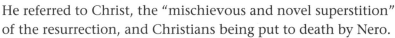

they be "examined" regarding their faith (similar to the response to Pliny the Younger).

Suetonius (circa A.D. 120)—A historian who wrote about events in the late 40s to 60s. He referred to Christ, the "mischievous and novel superstition" of the resurrection, and Christians being put to death by Nero.

Phlegon (circa A.D. 140)—Referenced by Julius Africanus and Origen, he referred to the "eclipse," the earthquake, and Jesus' prophecies.

Lucian of Samosata (circa A.D. 170)—This Greek satirist wrote about Christians, Christ, the crucifixion, Christian martyrs, and "novel beliefs."

Mara Bar-Serapion (before A.D. 200)—A Syrian philosopher, he wrote from prison to his son, comparing Jesus to Socrates and Plato.

Writings from Jewish Rabbis (circa A.D. 40-180)—Several passages from the Talmud and other Jewish writings clearly refer to Jesus Christ. References include:

- The "hanging" (on a cross) of Jesus on the eve of Passover.

- Identifying Jesus, along with the names of five of disciples.

- Healing in the name of Jesus.

- Scoffing at the "claim" that Jesus was born of a virgin, and implying His birth was probably "illegitimate."

Documentation Evidence

The position of Jewish scribe was one of the most demanding and esteemed jobs in biblical times. After training for years, scribes were allowed to practice the profession only after age 30. Often referred to as doctors of the Law, they joined the priests in teaching of the Law.

Scriptural Copy Rules[1]

Recording of holy Scripture was a serious responsibility. So important was the exact reproduction that Old Testament scribes were forced to adhere to demanding rules any time a manuscript was copied:

1. Scrolls—special paper, ink, and surface preparation were required.

2. Tight specifications—number of columns, 37 letters per column.

3. Master used—no duplicates of duplicates allowed.

4. Each letter—visually confirmed. No writing of phrases.

5. Distance between letters—checked with a thread.

6. Alphabet—each letter counted and compared to the original.

7. Letters per page—all were counted and compared to the master.

8. Middle letter of scroll—verified to be same as on the master.

9. One mistake—scroll was destroyed, if it was intended to be a master.

The Dead Sea Scrolls

Any doubt regarding the accurate transmission of manuscripts was erased in 1947 with the discovery of hundreds of scrolls buried for nearly 2000 years. Many were written before 100 B.C. Comparison with recent Jewish copies shows virtually no change.

First-Century Non-Biblical Writing

Many are unaware of the substantial amount of non-biblical early Christian writing about Jesus. In addition to thousands of fragments and letters referring to Jesus, other early manuscripts have been found that did not meet requirements for the New Testament. The *Gospel of Thomas* contains 114 sayings attributed to Jesus. Found in Egypt in 1946, it was probably written by the Gnostics, who followed a deviant cult-like philosophy condemned by the apostles. A *Gospel of Peter* dating back to the early second century was also recently found in Egypt. The writer identifies himself as Simon Peter and recounts events from the trial of Jesus to the resurrection. And an acrostic found at two sites in Pompeii (destroyed in A.D. 79) contains interesting symbolism. Jesus is referred to as "the sower," a common reference at the time. His deity is symbolized through a series of alphas and omegas separated by a "T" (or cross). And the word *tenet*, meaning "he holds," forms a central cross. This acrostic probably brought solace to the many undergoing extreme persecution at the time.

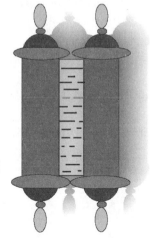

Did Jesus Perform Miracles?

The issue of Jesus performing miracles is hardly in doubt to anyone who studies the evidence—except of course to someone who doesn't believe miracles are possible in the first place.

Do Miracles Happen?

By definition, miracles are supernatural events, or things that cannot be reasonably explained by the natural laws of science. Denying miracles is like denying God. Hard-core skeptics are proud to insist that anything classified a miracle has a natural explanation. The problem, they say, is that we just haven't discovered the answer yet, as they cite things understood today that were considered miracles long ago. But even if we reject the thousands of miracles documented annually, no one can deny the world's existence—which required at least one creation miracle at the beginning. Albert Einstein, one of history's greatest skeptics, eventually accepted the existence of some kind of God.[2] And the general relativity equations proving his point are today accepted as fact by virtually all well-informed scientists. The Bible says we are "without excuse" (Romans 1:20).

In biblical days, there was far less skepticism regarding miracles. The bigger issue was who was responsible for the miracles, God or Satan. And the Bible indicates both are capable of miraculous "signs and wonders." According to the Bible, even miracles of "good" may be caused by Satan, who disguises himself as an "angel of light" (2 Corinthians 11:14). The miracles of Jesus differed in that they were performed to glorify God.

Jesus' Critics Have Acknowledged His Miracles

Although the enemies of Jesus tried to hide the resurrection (see pp. 20–23)—the ultimate prophetic proof of Jesus' deity—they did not deny Jesus as a miracle worker. Evidence within and even outside the Bible is extensive:

- *Jewish leaders knew of Jesus' miracles and asked Him to perform them.* They later claimed the miracles came from Satan, yet did *not* deny the miracles were real. Jesus pointed out that Satan would not "cast out Satan" and silenced His critics (Matthew 12:22-28).

- *Even Herod Antipas* knew of Jesus' miracles and wanted Him to perform them (Matthew 14:1,2; Mark 6:14; Luke 23:8).

- *Non-Christian history further confirms Jesus' miracles.* Historians of the first two centuries wrote matter-of-factly about Jesus' miracles. Such authors included Josephus and Jewish rabbis.

A Chronology of Jesus' Miracles

Thorough analysis suggests it may be more difficult to reject evidence of miracles than to accept it. Unlike some people who claim to be "miracle workers," Jesus had *many people witness* His acts. When the Gospel accounts were later recorded, eyewitnesses would be able to challenge the credibility of the events. A summary of the witnessed miracles includes:

MIRACLE	WITNESSES
• **Water turned into wine** (John 2:1-11)	*Wedding guests*
• **Boy in Capernaum healed** (John 4:46-55)	*Man, servant*
• **Miraculous catch of fish—first time** (Luke 5:1-11)	*Crowd*
• **Evil spirit sent out** (Mark 1:23-27)	*Synagogue*
• **Peter's mother-in-law healed** (Matthew 8:14-17; Mark 1:29-31; Luke 4:38,39)	*Five people*
• **Leper is healed** (Matthew 8:1-4, Mark 1:40-45; Luke 5:12-15)	*Many people*
• **Paralytic healed** (Matthew 9:1,2; Mark 2:1-5; Luke 5:17-26)	*"So many"*
• **Lame man healed** (John 5:1-3)	*"A great number"*
• **Shriveled hand restored** (Matthew 12:9-14; Mark 3:1-6; Luke 6:1-11)	*Pharisees*
• **Heals many** (Matthew 12:15-21; Mark 3:7-12)	*"Many people"*
• **Centurion's slave healed** (Matthew 8:5-13; Luke 7:1-10)	*Elders, friends*
• **Widow's son resurrected** (Luke 7:11-17)	*Large crowd*
• **Crippled woman healed** (Luke 13:10-17)	*Synagogue and ruler*
• **Calming of the sea** (Matthew 8:23-27; Mark 4:35-41; Luke 8:22-25)	*Disciples*
• **Demons sent into pigs** (Matthew 8:28-34; Mark 5:1-20; Luke 8:26-39)	*Town and country*

Witnessed by thousands, the miracles all took place in a brief 3½ years.

- **Sick woman healed**   *Large crowd*
  (Matthew 9:20-22; Mark 5:25-34; Luke 8:43-48)

- **Jairus' daughter resurrected**   *Synagogue*
  (Matthew 9:23-26; Mark 5:35-43; Luke 8:49-56)

- **Two blind men healed**   *Region "told"*
  (Matthew 9:27-31)

- **Mute made to speak**   *Crowd*
  (Matthew 9:32-34)

- **5000 fed**   *5000 People*
  (Matthew 14:15-21; Mark 6:35-44; Luke 9:10-17; John 6:5-14)

- **Walks on water**   *Disciples*
  (Matthew 14:22-33; Mark 6:45-51; John 6:17-21)

- **Girl freed from demon**   *Woman*
  (Matthew 15:21-28; Mark 7:24-30)

- **Deaf mute healed**   *"Some people"*
  (Mark 7:31-37)

- **4000 fed**   *4000 People*
  (Matthew 15:29-39; Mark 8:1-10)

- **Blind man healed**   *Some people*
  (Mark 8:22-26)

- **Boy healed from demon**   *Large crowd*
  (Matthew 17:14-21; Mark 9:14-29; Luke 9:37-42)

- **Coin from fish's mouth**   *Tax collectors*
  (Matthew 17:24-27)

- **Man born blind healed**   *Neighbors, others*
  (John 9:1-12)

- **Ten lepers healed**   *Samaritans*
  (Luke 17:11-19)

- **Man with dropsy healed**   *Pharisees, others*
  (Luke 14:1-6)

- **Lazarus raised from the dead**   *Jews, family*
  (John 11:1-45)

- **Blind Bartimaeus healed**   *Large crowd*
  (Matthew 20:29-34; Mark 10:46-52; Luke 18:35-43)

- **Fig tree cursed**   *Disciples*
  (Matthew 21:18-22; Mark 11:20-26)

- **Soldier's ear healed**   *Group*
  (Matthew 26:50-54; Mark 14:46,47; Luke 22:49-51; John 18:10,11)

Did the Resurrection Occur?

As prior pages indicate, the crucifixion of Jesus was especially well documented and accepted as fact. The crucial question then becomes: Did Jesus rise from the dead, proving His claim to be God incarnate, or did something else happen with His body—or was He never dead at all?

A key to this issue is the extreme *local importance* placed on handling this execution. Powerful, insightful speaking and many miracles had led the populace to request that Jesus become king. This began to threaten the local political stability of the Romans and the religious power of the Jewish leaders whom Jesus openly criticized. Both the absolute death of Jesus and the prevention of a hoax were critical, since Jesus had claimed He would overcome death. Furthermore, He had already raised others from the dead. As a result, all precautions were taken (Matthew 27:62-66).

The Bible implies the cause of Jesus' death was cardiac arrest—indicated by blood and water pouring from a spear wound (medical experts confirm this). To secure the body, a Roman guard was placed outside the tomb. Such a guard would have consisted of 16 soldiers, with a disciplined rotation for sleeping at night—every four hours four guards would switch. The guards all faced the rigid Roman penalty of crucifixion for sleeping outside of the assigned shift or deserting their post. The idea that all guards were asleep, considering the death penalty, is especially unreasonable. To further ensure safekeeping, a two-ton stone[1] was rolled in front of the tomb with Pontius Pilate's seal on it. Breaking the seal without the official Roman guard's approval meant crucifixion upside down. The central issue—unexplainable by Jewish leaders, especially in light of the many precautions—is:

What happened to Jesus' corpse if He did not rise from the dead as indicated in the Gospel accounts?

The official explanation is that the disciples stole the body while the guards were asleep (with the priests protecting the guards from the governor). This idea was necessary only because *no one could produce a dead body of Jesus* . . . which would have stopped the resurrection story forever. Is a theft of Jesus' body even remotely possible?

- *All 16 guards would have had to risk the penalty of crucifixion* by sleeping or deserting. Surely at least one guard would have been awake.

- *The disciples were in a state of shock, fear and disarray,* having seen their Master crucified. Is it reasonable to think they quickly created a brilliant plan and flawlessly executed it on the Sabbath day of rest?

- *What possible motive could the disciples have had?* If Jesus was not the Son of God as He claimed, stealing the body would have created a lie with no apparent benefit—and death, *for no purpose*, for the disciples.

Analysis of Other Explanations

Was Jesus really dead? Crucifixion was more routine, and was physically draining for a longer period, than the electric chair today. Is it likely such professional executioners did not recognize death? The final spear thrust to the heart area was to ensure the person was dead. For such a political threat, they would be certain. If Jesus was not dead, what are the chances that a barely living person could move a two-ton rock from the inside of a tomb and escape a full Roman guard unnoticed?

Was the body stolen at night? Recognizing that no flashlights or infrared sensors were available then, is it likely that a band of scared disciples carrying torches could bypass a full Roman guard, move a two-ton rock and not be noticed? Furthermore, the two Sabbaths greatly limited movement. And again—for what motive?

Eyewitnesses to the Truth Died to Tell the Story

Martyrdom for a belief is not unique. But what kind of person would die for a *known* lie? Someone insane? Would *all* the disciples face hardship and death for a known lie? The disciples were with Jesus constantly for three years. They would certainly have known the truth of the resurrection. Lying would serve no purpose since Jesus' ministry would then be moot. Yet historical records and reports about the disciples indicated they all died cruel deaths for their beliefs (except John). James was *stoned*, Peter *crucified* upside down, Paul *beheaded*, Thaddaeus killed by *arrows*, Matthew and James (son of Zebedee) killed by the *sword*, and others *crucified*.

The Testimony of the Catacombs

Underneath Rome lie some 900 miles of carved caves where more than 7 million Christians, many executed for their beliefs, were buried. Others hid and worshiped in these caves during the height of Christian persecution. The earliest known inscriptions in the walls were dated A.D. 70. Some early occupants probably communicated directly with people who had seen Jesus. From about A.D. 400 the Catacombs were buried and "forgotten" for more than 1000 years. In 1578 they were rediscovered by accident. Today they can be seen as silent memorials to many who died rather than curse Jesus or bow down to an emperor's statue. Christian martyrs differed greatly from other world martyrs in that *historical facts were the foundation of beliefs—facts verifiable at the time, not just ideas.*

Hostile Witnesses Turn Christian

Paul, a leading executioner of Christians, gave up wealth, power, and comfort upon seeing the resurrected Christ, then wrote most of the New Testament. Two Sanhedrin members (not present when the Sanhedrin sentenced Jesus to death) were secret disciples. Unbelieving natural brothers of Jesus, James and Jude, later became believers—*after the resurrection.*

Courts of law regard hostile witnesses as very important since their natural inclination is to dispute facts favorable to their opponent. The Bible makes it clear that hostile witnesses became believers in Jesus.

The Prophecies—Statistical "Proof"

Although history can never be "proven," enormous statistical probability is often viewed as "proof" by scientists and mathematicians. God's involvement in the life of Jesus is statistically "certain."

As indicated earlier, the prophecies contained in the Old Testament were written long before Jesus' birth. The Dead Sea Scrolls provide irrefutable evidence that the accounts were not tampered with over the centuries. Of the 469 historical prophecies contained in the Old Testament that would have been fulfilled, 467 have been verified as fulfilled (we have no record of fulfillment of two). Perhaps the most fascinating prophecies are those regarding Jesus.

Prophecies About Jesus

Who

Ancestors prophesied:

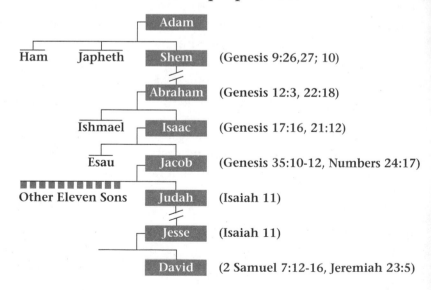

Adam	
Ham Japheth Shem	(Genesis 9:26,27; 10)
Abraham	(Genesis 12:3, 22:18)
Ishmael Isaac	(Genesis 17:16, 21:12)
Esau Jacob	(Genesis 35:10-12, Numbers 24:17)
Other Eleven Sons Judah	(Isaiah 11)
Jesse	(Isaiah 11)
David	(2 Samuel 7:12-16, Jeremiah 23:5)

What

The life and role of Jesus also were precisely recorded in prophecy written hundreds of years before His birth. The descriptions of what Jesus would become include the miraculous elements of His birth, His divine nature, and details of His earthly life. The Scriptures prophesied that:

1. A virgin would be with child. (Isaiah 7:14)

2. The child would be God, not a normal human being. The name Immanuel literally means "God with us." (Isaiah 7:14)

3. The One who was born would be an eternal Savior. (Isaiah 9:6,7)

4. The Savior would be for both the Jews and the Gentiles. (Isaiah 49:6)

5. He would work many miracles, including making the deaf hear, the blind see, the lame walk, and the mute speak. (Isaiah 29:18; 35:5,6)

6. He would suffer greatly. (Isaiah 53)

7. He would be crucified for human transgressions. (Isaiah 53:5)

8. He would bear the sin of many and be made an intercessor. (Isaiah 53:12)

9. He would be rejected by His own people, the Jews. (Isaiah 53:3; Psalm 118:22; Matthew 21:42-46)

When

Prophecy of the date of Palm Sunday

(Daniel 9:20-27) Although complex until understood, this prophecy, made about 535 B.C., predicted Jesus' final entry into Jerusalem to the day. The prophecy states:

Daniel's "Seventy Sevens"

- Sixty-nine periods of 7 (years) will pass from the decree to rebuild Jerusalem until the coming of the "Anointed One" ("Messiah" in Hebrew). This dates Jesus' entry into Jerusalem on Palm Sunday.

- After that time the Anointed One will be cut off (Hebrew "yikaret," meaning a sudden, violent end—crucifixion).

- And after that time the city and the temple will be destroyed.

> Daniel, a Hebrew, received the prophetic revelation in 535 B.C.
> Using the Hebrew definition of year (360 days), we find:
> 69 x 7 years = 173,880 days.

The actual decree to rebuild Jerusalem was given by Artaxerxes[3] on March 14, 445 B.C. (first day of Nisan that year—Nehemiah 2:1-6).

Using the actual 365-day calendar along with adjustments for leap years, and the final scientific adjustment (leap year dropped every 128 years), we find this number of days brings us precisely to:[4]

April 6, A.D. 32

History: Jesus' ministry began in the fifteenth year of Tiberius Caesar (Luke 3:1), whose reign began in A.D. 14. A chronological analysis of Jesus' ministry shows three years leading up to the final week, in A.D. 32.

The Royal Observatory in Greenwich, England, confirms the Sunday before Passover that year to be:

April 6, A.D. 32

Other prophecy elements were fulfilled as well:

- Jesus was crucified $3^{1}/_{2}$ days later.
- The Romans destroyed the city and the temple in A.D. 70.

Where

Precise city of Jesus' birth

The Bible (Micah 5:2) specified that Jesus would be born in Bethlehem, in Ephrathah (that is, in Judea—there was another Bethlehem closer to Joseph's home in Nazareth).

Other Prophecies

- King on a donkey (Zechariah 9:9)

- Suffers, is rejected (Isaiah 53:1-3)

- Crucified, pierced (Psalm 22:16)

- Lots cast for clothing (Psalm 22:18)

- No bones broken (Psalm 22:17)

- Given gall and wine (Psalm 69:20-22)

- Pierced with a spear (Zechariah 12:10)

- Posterity to serve Him (Psalm 22:30)

- Betrayed by friend (Psalm 41:9)

- For 30 pieces of silver (Zechariah 11:13)

- Silver cast on temple floor, used to buy potter's field (Zechariah 11:13)

Experts in statistics estimate the probability of all these prophecies coming true in ANY one man is about one chance in 10^{99}—less than the odds of correctly selecting one electron out of all the matter in the universe—or essentially zero without divine intervention.[1]

Jesus—Was He God?

Christians claim that Jesus was in reality God appearing to the world in human flesh. The Christian concept of the one God of the universe includes three distinctly different yet inextricable parts: the Father, the Son (Jesus), and the Holy Spirit. Though this is somewhat difficult to understand, analogies have been made to H_2O, which can exist as water, ice, and vapor; and to light, which has the physical properties of both waves and particles.

Did Jesus Think He Was God?

Many times Jesus referred to His own deity, both directly and indirectly. Although Jesus confirmed that He was the Messiah (Mark 14:62,63) He did not use the term "Messiah" to refer to Himself—perhaps to differentiate His deity from the widespread expectation of a human Messiah. Jesus used the terms *Son of Man* and *Son of God* often. Both referred to His divine nature (Daniel 7:13,14; Matthew 26:63,64). Jesus also used the specific words "I am" (*Ego eimi* in Greek, *Ani bu* in Hebrew) on several occasions (see John 8:56-58). God used these same words to describe Himself to Moses. Jesus also stated specifically that He and God "are one" (John 10:30).

And Jesus clearly indicated He had authority over issues controlled only by God, such as forgiveness of sin (Mark 2:5-10). Also divine were the timeless power of His words (Matthew 24:35) and His glory (John 17:5). Perhaps as significant was Jesus' acceptance of worship (Luke 5:8; John 20:28). The intense monotheistic foundation of the Jews would absolutely forbid any worship of anything but the one true God. Overall analysis of Jesus' life—His compassionate miracles, His perfect lifestyle, and His love—indicates that His claims alone are trustworthy, and are perhaps the strongest evidence of His divinity.

Did Others Think of Jesus as God?

The disciples clearly came to view Jesus as God in human flesh, and they worshiped Him as such (Luke 5:8; John 20:28). Certainly the witnessing of the resurrection and the transfiguration (Matthew 17:1) provided irrefutable evidence to them. New Testament and early Christian writing define Jesus as God—our Lord—here on earth (1 Corinthians 8:6; 1 Timothy 2:5).

What Other Evidence Is There of Jesus' Deity?

Many say Jesus' miracles are evidence of His deity. But miracles have been recorded as being performed by others (in the Bible and elsewhere). The Bible states that perfect fulfillment of prophecy proves God's intervention (Deuteronomy 18:21,22). The odds of all Old Testament prophecies about Jesus coming true in any one man are beyond statistical possibility without divine intervention (see pp. 24–27). And Jesus prophesied with perfect accuracy regarding such things as the precise timing of His death, the exact manner of His death, His resurrection, and His later appearance in Galilee. Prophetic perfection and a claim to be God together verify Jesus' deity.

Jesus—What Was His Purpose?

Although Jesus' life served many purposes, the Bible is clear that the main, overwhelming purpose of His visit was to become a sacrifice—offering forgiveness and eternal life to all who establish the right relationship with God through Jesus. (John 3:16; John 17:1-5)

The Old Testament contains a complete summary of the relationship God seeks with man. It includes specific laws, and defines the sacrifices that must be made when laws are broken. Further, it provides a history of man's failure to meet God's standards, ultimately resulting in God's judgment. Perhaps most important, the Old Testament points to the ultimate solution for a creation bent on falling short of God's commands. The solution was a promised Messiah, an "Anointed One," a Savior.

God's own requirement for atonement for sin involved a blood sacrifice of a "perfect" unblemished animal (Leviticus 4 and 5). God didn't require that people go out and "do good things" to make up for sin. He required a blood sacrifice. And His forgiveness was based on grace alone.

Why Do We Need a Savior?

It may seem irrational that God would place a requirement on His creation that would necessitate sacrificing His own Son. Even so, people are born with the instinct that sin requires a sacrifice to obtain forgiveness. Laws in virtually any society reflect this instinct. When people violate traffic laws, they are given a ticket and sacrifice money. If more serious laws are broken, they sacrifice time—in jail. Even the most evil people, assuming the role of a god, force others to "pay" (maybe through torture or murder) when they believe they are "wronged." Whether their interpretation is rational or not, people seem to understand the concept of sacrifice for sin. Perhaps God created this concept—even though it ultimately required His own painful and sacrificial fulfillment—just so he could demonstrate how very great His love is for the world (John 3:16).

While it may be difficult to understand sacrifice as the payment for sin, it's not difficult to understand why human beings need forgiveness. God's standard is perfect goodness. And even the most righteous fall well short of such a standard. Acts of an individual may appear pure and perfect. But enter the mind of the same person and you will find hate, envy, lust, and any number of other thoughts regarded as sin by God (Matthew 5:28).

Jesus' Other Purposes

- To provide relief to the oppressed (Luke 4:18-20)

- To teach God's nature and commands (Matthew 4:23)

- To prophesy the future of the world (Revelation 1:1-3)

How Is Jesus Different?

Religious leaders abound. What facts separate Jesus from all the others? Four things make Jesus especially unique: 1) His claim to be a person of the One God—verified by prophecy and His resurrection, 2) His literal fulfillment of prophecy contained in preexisting holy documents, 3) His performance of many miracles, 4) His own various prophecies and their precise fulfillment.

Jesus: A Claim to Be One God—Verified by His Prophecy and Resurrection

Jesus claimed to be God on several occasions (see p. 28). This makes Him unique among religious leaders. He prophesied about His death and resurrection. He then died and rose from the dead, just as He predicted.

Compare this to other leaders of large religions. Hinduism had no known leader to compare to Jesus. Buddha and Confucius *never* claimed to be God at all (although both were deified by some followers later). Muhammad (founder of Islam) *never* claimed to be God. None of these world religious leaders are revered for miracles, for prophecy fulfilled, or for provable prophesies they themselves made. All died and stayed dead.

Joseph Smith (founder of Mormonism), Mary Baker Eddy (founder of Christian Science), and other leaders of large religions who are considered to be god in some sense all fall far short of Jesus. None have fulfilled historical (provable) prophecy. None have successfully proclaimed significant prophecy themselves. And all have died and stayed dead.

Jesus: Fulfillment of Prophecy in Preexisting Holy Documents

Jesus often declared that he was the One of whom Jewish holy Scripture and prophecy spoke (see Matthew 16:13-20; Mark 12:10-13). Jewish Scripture was widely recognized and was considered holy for many centuries. The theme of a Messiah (or Savior) was woven throughout Scripture with highly detailed prophecies. Jesus fit the descriptions precisely. Both Jesus and His disciples used many examples to back this claim.

Other leaders such as Buddha, Confucius, Muhammad, and Mary Baker Eddy wrote (or dictated) their own holy writings, so there was no opportunity to be tested by previous holy prophecy. Joseph Smith claimed his Book of Mormon to be a divine translation from ancient "golden plates." However there is absolutely no evidence of the plates, nor even any evidence of the information contained in the Book of Mormon. The Smithsonian Institution has flatly rejected it as history.

Jesus: Performance of Many Miracles

The many miracles of Jesus contained in the Gospels were confirmed as literal by hundreds of eyewitnesses who accepted the widely circulated Gospel records. The eyewitnesses later faced martyrdom as a result of their strong belief. Jesus' miracles included making blind people see, making deaf people hear, and making lame people walk. These miracles had also been predicted of the Messiah centuries in advance (see Isaiah 35:4-6). Even non-Christian historians wrote about Jesus' reputation as a miracle worker (for example Josephus and Jewish rabbis—see p. 12–13).

No other religious founder offers historical evidence of an abundance of widely accepted miracles. And certainly no historical documentation exists for anyone raising someone from the dead, apart from Jesus (see Matthew 9:18-26; John 11:38-44).

Jesus: Precise Historical Prophecy

Prophecy—100 percent accurately fulfilled—is the absolute test of whether something is from God. Jesus predicted His crucifixion to the exact day (at the last supper), the betrayal by a friend (identified specifically at the last supper), the three denials by Peter, the resurrection (defining the exact day), the coming of the Holy Spirit, and the establishment of the Church. All of this was described in historical accounts verified by eyewitnesses.

No other religious founder offers such amazing historical (that is, testable) prophecy.

Was Jesus Just a Good Teacher or Prophet?

People often want to reject Jesus' claim to be God, yet feel compelled to acknowledge Him historically, as a good teacher or prophet.

Why?

Accepting Jesus as God implies accepting His teaching and prophecy. This makes some people *very* uncomfortable. After all, people don't want to love, forgive, and pray for their enemies. Nor do they want to humble themselves or become servants. And some people are caught up in a lifestyle that Jesus teaches against. Perhaps such people believe they can justify disobedience if Jesus is not God.

Jesus: A Good Teacher?

Could Jesus be a good teacher if all of His teachings were wrong? The religious teachers scoffed at Jesus' teaching because it often contradicted the multitude of laws they had added to Scripture. Yet it was *strictly scripturally based*. Today some reject Jesus because His teaching contradicts what they want to do or believe. Jesus' teaching goal was never to be a popular teacher. It was to teach the truth. Jesus also taught that He was God. Was He a good teacher? Or a fool? Or a liar?

Jesus: A Good Prophet?

Today we will call almost anyone a prophet. Correctly predict the score of a football game, and someone might call you a prophet—no matter how many times you've failed. People like

Jesus—Mocked as a Prophet

When Jesus was being tortured by soldiers before crucifixion, they mocked His claim to be God by asking Him to prophesy (Mark 14:65). The soldiers were aware that 100-percent accurate prophecy was considered a sign of God for the Jews.

Nostradamus, Jeane Dixon, and Edgar Cayce are all called prophets (by tabloid reporters and others) despite the fact that most of their predictions were wrong.

In biblical times, prophecy in the name of God was considered extremely seriously. In fact, if a prophet made just one prophecy that did not come true, he was put to death by stoning (see Deuteronomy 18:20). So could Jesus be a good prophet and also be wrong? *No!* He was one or the other. Ironically, many of today's Jewish teachers who cherish Old Testament laws also call Jesus a good prophet—while still rejecting His prophecies (especially His resurrection prophecies). They are contradicting themselves.

Why Should We Accept Jesus as God?

Some people think that believing in Jesus and being good are the secret to heaven. The Bible says otherwise. It says that religion, speaking in Jesus' name, and being good are of no value if Jesus doesn't *know* us (see Matthew 7:21-23). Knowing Jesus is more than just a belief about Jesus. It means repenting and accepting Jesus' sacrifice and His claims to be God.

Jesus Shows God's Love for Us

We are all separated from God by imperfection. Even the most righteous people have had unholy thoughts considered sinful by God (see Matthew 5:28). Since God is *perfect* and holy, His requirement for an eternal, heavenly relationship with Him is perfection that no human can ever offer. So God provided an alternative method to rejoin us with Himself through one perfect sacrifice, forgiving all of our imperfections. The only way for God to have such a perfect sacrifice was for God to fulfill it Himself. By sending His Spirit into Mary (Luke 1:35), God essentially came to earth in human form as Jesus, to be sacrificed and show His love for mankind (see John 3:16). To fully appreciate God's love, we need to be aware of the excruciating pain and humility Jesus willingly suffered for many who hated (or now hate) Him.

Rejecting Jesus Shows Our Disdain for God

Jesus can be rejected in two ways: 1) by a decision to reject Him or 2) by simply not accepting Him. Knowing about Jesus, even believing the gospel story, is not *accepting* Him nor showing love for God. Even demons and Satan believe the gospel (see Mark 5:6-17). Love for God means *acceptance* of Jesus. It means turning our lives over to Him for guidance. The Greek word used in the

God's Unaccepted Gift?

Imagine sending your only child to deliver a gift to show forgiveness to an adversary. Imagine knowing that your child would die painfully while delivering it. Now suppose that person never opened the gift—never accepting forgiveness. Would you choose to be with him forever?

Bible for "believe" (as in John 3:16) is *pisteuö,* which literally means to *trust,* or *have faith in.* This means more than intellectual knowledge. Imagine the disdain we show God by not accepting His very precious and loving sacrifice.

Acceptance or Rejection Is for Eternity

The Bible frequently reveals God's judgment. This does not conflict with God's love and forgiveness, most emphatically shown through the sacrifice of His Son. But it does reveal that God is *just.* In the end, the Bible clearly states that there will be a separation of those who trusted Jesus as God, and those who didn't. This separation is forever (see Luke 13:23-30; Revelation 20:12-15).

What Will "Knowing" Jesus Do?

It's natural to ask how a relationship will benefit us. A relationship with Jesus promises many things. But as in any relationship, as it matures, our focus will shift more to what we can do for Jesus, rather than what He can do for us.

Benefits of Knowing Jesus

Freedom—Psychologists tell us that guilt is one of the leading causes of stress in the world today. Fear is another. So freedom from guilt and anxiety alone might be reason enough to accept the Word of God about Jesus. Jesus said that He is the "truth" (John 14:6), and that "knowing the truth" would set us free (John 8:32)—furthermore, that His yoke is easy and His burden is light (Matthew 11:30). The Bible also gives vivid examples of why we need not worry about the future (Matthew 6:26-34). These promises confirm that a relationship with Jesus will bring freedom from the burdens of life.

Such freedom is conditioned upon accepting God's forgiveness. People sometimes don't realize the extent of forgiveness God offers. Yet He forgives even murderers and adulterers, such as King David and Moses. Paul, a zealous murderer of Christians, found Jesus and became the leading author of the New Testament and a founder of the Christian church. Freedom doesn't mean that problems won't occur in life; they will, just as with everyone else (Paul faced incredible problems). What the Bible does promise is a new freedom and strength to face problems.

Heaven—The central reason for God's sending Christ to earth was for man to have a path to redemption from sin, and eternal life in heaven with God (John 3:16). This message is so vital that it is referred to frequently throughout the Bible, and it is central to every book in the New Testament.

Joy and Peace—Once we understand that we have freedom in Christ, and we fully realize that our *eternal life in paradise is certain,* we can experience incredible joy and peace in spite of any kind of trouble. The Bible refers to this as peace that surpasses all understanding (Philippians 4:6,7).

Specifically, What Can God Do?

Although it would be a mistake to think of God as some sort of magic power to be called upon to accomplish our wishes, God does promise that He will meet our needs (not our wants). And God has the power to do anything within His will. Such things include:

- Healing the sick and broken-hearted.

- Providing for material and financial needs.

- Giving strength to resist temptation and addictions.

- Repairing and strengthening relationships.

- Defining our purpose in life.

Why Do People Reject Jesus?

The evidence regarding Jesus is so overwhelming that it seems incredible that many people still reject Him. After all, the promises of a better life on earth and eternal life in heaven are not bad promises, and they're easy and free. Rejection of the Messiah, however, should not be surprising. It was often prophesied (Isaiah 53:1-3; Psalm 118:22; Matthew 21:42-46; Luke 16:19-31).

Ignorance—Perhaps the greatest reason for non-belief in Jesus is ignorance. Most people take far too little time to investigate their religious beliefs. As a result, world opinion often becomes the basis for the most important issue in life. It may come from a family belief, friends, or a dominant church in the community. But in the end, it doesn't matter what the reason is if you are wrong. Nor does sincerity matter. As history has shown all too often, people can be very sincere, yet sincerely wrong.

Apathy—Many times people have a false sense of security that God will take care of everyone. This idea is sometimes accompanied with the thought that hell doesn't exist, or that God will send everyone who "tries to be good" to heaven anyway. This is *not* what the Bible teaches. The Bible reveals that God's promises are reserved for His people and there are many reasons why others "don't hear" (Matthew 13:11-43). The reality and horror of hell are clearly stated, including the narrowness of the path to get to heaven (Matthew 7:13).

Fear—Some people fear that becoming a Christian means "giving up fun" or living a strange, secluded life without friends. Nowhere in the Bible does it say we must start a dull life and turn away from having parties with other people. It says the opposite. The Bible promises that knowing Jesus will let us "live life to the fullest" (John 10:10). And not only will such freedom draw us to have fun with friends; the Bible says even the angels in heaven "throw a party" when we accept Jesus as Lord (Luke 15:10).

Tradition—People tend to adopt their parent's beliefs, even if they're wrong. This reason for rejecting Jesus is often the strongest. But we are each accountable for our own actions. Even society doesn't send parents to jail for their children's crimes. Jesus knew He would, at times, cause people to break away from traditional family beliefs (Matthew 10:21,22).

The Influence of Evil

Fully understanding why people reject Jesus requires recognizing the existence of supernatural agents of evil, every bit as real as God and agents of good. The Bible extensively acknowledges demons, Satan, and deceitful evil influence. The goal of evil is to do whatever it takes to draw people away from Jesus. One step off the path is all it takes, such as a different "kind" of Jesus or a stubborn resistance to asking Him to direct our life. And the world is filled with such evil trying to draw us away. But sincerely asking God to reveal the truth will overcome it (see page 46).

Answers to Common Questions

How Do We Know the Bible Is Accurate?

First, the integrity of original biblical manuscripts has been demonstrated by the vast number of manuscripts precisely copied during the time of eyewitnesses and verified as unchanged by the Dead Sea Scrolls (see pp. 10,11,15). Secondly, archaeology has shown the Bible's complete consistency with what we know as history of the world. Third, hundreds of ancient prophecies contained in the Bible, showing 100-percent accuracy, indicate divine guidance (see pp. 24–27). And finally, the Bible is 100 percent consistent with established facts of science . . . which is corroborated by many of the finest scientists in the world today.

Why Do Some People Claim the Bible Has Contradictions?

After hundreds of years of challenge, the accuracy of the Bible has stood the test of time. Common types of misunderstandings include:

1. *Details that once seemed to contradict science or archaeology.* Often our information is too limited for us to know that the Bible is right. For many years scholars believed the earth was flat, while the Bible indicated a spherical shape. Likewise, critics scoffed at the mention of the early Hittites, or cities like Sodom and Gomorrah . . . all thought to be non-existent, yet verified as fact today. Scientists have recently "proven" Einstein's definition of the universe (consistent with the Bible), which has superseded Newton's more limited view. The list goes on and on. As archaeology and science reveal more, the Bible is verified and has yet to be proved wrong.

QA

2. *Different accounts by different authors.*
    Details contained in different Gospels
    may at first seem contradictory. How-
    ever the accounts simply report
    events from different vantage points.
    For example, Matthew records that Mary Magdalene and "the
    other Mary" went to the tomb. Mark records Mary
    Magdalene and Mary, mother of James, and Salome. Luke
    records "the women", and John records Mary Magdalene. Are
    the reports contradictory? No. Different people reported dif-
    ferent facts. Placed side by side, they just give a more
    complete picture of what happened.

The Chronological Visit to the Tomb[5]

The three women went to the tomb and saw a "young man" who
told them of the resurrection and also told them to go tell the
disciples. They left and returned with Peter and John, who
viewed the tomb. The disciples then returned home, and the
women stayed. At that time Jesus appeared to Mary Magdalene.

As with witnesses to an event today, when all testimony is pieced
together, it makes perfect sense and a more complete picture is
given.

Are Heaven and Hell Real?

The Bible extensively reviews heaven, hell, Satan, angels, and demons—all found in many of its 66 books. Surveys show that many more people believe in heaven than in hell. Some non-biblical religions even deny that hell exists. Yet Jesus actually spoke more about hell than about heaven. So it would not be wise to ignore hell. Jesus gives us a very pointed warning regarding heaven and hell (Luke 16:19-31).

What the Bible Says About Heaven and Hell

Heaven	Hell
Wonderful (2 Corinthians 12:1–4)	**Eternal torment** (Mark 9:43–49)
Worth giving up all (Matthew 13:44–46)	**Separation from God** (Luke 16:19–31)
A place where God dwells (Deuteronomy 26:15)	**A place where Satan dwells** (Revelation 20:10)
Perfect—no pain (Revelation 21:1–4)	**Full of sorrow** (2 Peter 2:4–9)

It would *seem* wonderful if there was only a path to heaven with no hell. Not surprisingly, false prophets attempting to design religion according to people's desires try to do away with hell, or convince people that they can become a God. The Bible is specific concerning the path to heaven, and indicates that other paths lead to hell.

How Do We Know Which Religion Is Right?

No religion is "right" in and of itself. The Bible is about man's relationship with God—the right way and the wrong way. Any religion that is totally consistent with the Bible's teaching is right. Any that is counter to it is wrong.

So the reliability of the Bible as a guideline is vital. As indicated, the original biblical manuscripts are a miracle in and of themselves. Evidence of reliability includes: 1) an explosion of credible, corroborative writing, 2) verifiability *at the time* by eyewitnesses, 3) eyewitnesses dying for testimony they could affirm to be true, and 4) many other people, able to know historical facts, also dying for the same beliefs. If the New Testament is true, then the Old Testament is also broadly verified by Jesus (Luke 16:16,17), by more than 700 cross-references, by the Dead Sea Scrolls evidence, and by "mathematical proof" of hundreds of prophecies.

A problem arises when people start changing or adding to the Bible. Several things would indicate that such "inspiration" is not from God. First, the Bible commands us not to add to, delete, or change it (Revelation 22:18,19). Secondly, Jesus verified it would not change (Luke 16:17). And third, why would a perfect God change His original, perfect Word?

The Bible is very clear that the path to heaven is defined as Christ:

| John 14:6–9 | Matthew 27:51–53 | John 3:16 | John 5:18–24 |
| Acts 4:12 | Colossians 1:15–23 | John 6:48–58 | Hebrews 10:26–31 |

Avoiding False Gods—The Bible warns against the following false gods:

- A god that is *not* a *single* God of the universe (having *no* peers—including humans) is *not* the God of the Bible (1 Timothy 2:5; Isaiah 44:6).

- A god *not* manifest as God the Father, God the Son, and God the Holy Spirit is *not* the God of the Bible (Luke 12:8-10; John 1:1,2,14; Acts 5:3,4).

- A god that does *not* proclaim Jesus Christ as the ultimate sacrifice for redemption of those committing themselves to Him is *not* the God of the Bible (Matthew 27:51-53; Mark 14:24; John 6:48-58; Acts 4:12; Colossians 1:15-23).

How Can We Ensure the Right Relationship to Go to Heaven?

When Jesus said not all who use His name will enter heaven (Matthew 7:21-23), He was referring to people who think using Christ's name along with rituals and rules is the key to heaven. A *relationship* with God is *not* based on rituals and rules. It's based on grace and forgiveness, and the right kind of relationship with Him.

How to Have a Personal Relationship with God

1. **B**elieve that God exists and that He came to earth in the human form of Jesus Christ (John 3:16; Romans 10:9).

2. **A**ccept God's free forgiveness of sins through the death and resurrection of Jesus Christ (Ephesians 2:8-10; 1:7,8).

3. **S**witch to God's plan for life (1 Peter 1:21-23; Ephesians 2:1-5).

4. **E**xpress desire for Christ to be director of your life (Matthew 7:21-27; 1 John 4:15).

Prayer for Eternal Life with God

"Dear God, I believe You sent Your Son, Jesus, to die for my sins so I can be forgiven. I'm sorry for my sins, and I want to live the rest of my life the way You want me to. Please put Your Spirit in my life to direct me. Amen."

Then What?

People who have taken the previous steps automatically become members of God's family of believers. A new world of freedom and strength is then available through prayer and obedience to God's will. New believers also can build their relationship with God by taking the following steps:

- Find a Bible-based church that you like, and attend regularly.

- Try to set aside some time each day to pray and read the Bible.

- Locate other Christians to spend time with on a regular basis.

God's Promises to Believers

For Today

But seek first his kingdom and his righteousness, and all these things [that is, things to satisfy all your needs] will be given to you as well.
—Matthew 6:33

For Eternity

Whoever believes in the Son has eternal life, but whoever rejects the Son will not see life, for God's wrath remains on him.
—John 3:36

Once we develop an eternal perspective, even the greatest problems on earth fade in significance.

Notes

1. McDowell, Josh and Wilson, Bill. *A Ready Defense*. San Bernardino, CA: Here's Life Publishers, Inc., 1990.

2. Ross, Hugh, Ph.D. *The Fingerprint of God*. Orange, CA: Promise Publishing Co., 1989.

3. *Encyclopedia Britannica*. Chicago, IL: 1993.

4. Rosen, Moishe. *Y'shua*. Chicago, IL: Moody Bible Institute, 1982.

5. Smith, F. LaGard. *The Daily Bible in Chronological Order*. Eugene, OR: Harvest House, 1984.

Bibliography

Encyclopedia Britannica, Chicago, IL: 1993.

Free, Joseph P. and Vos, Howard F. *Archaeology and Bible History*. Grand Rapids, MI: Zondervan, 1969.

Green, Michael, *Who Is This Jesus?* Nashville, TN: Thomas Nelson Publishers, 1992.

Josephus, Flavius. *The Complete Works of Josephus*, Translated by Whiston, Wm. Grand Rapids, MI: Kregel, 1981.

Keely, Robin. *Jesus 2000*. Batavia, IL: Lion Publishing plc, 1989.

MacArthur, John F. Jr. *God With Us*. Grand Rapids, MI. Zondervan Publishing House, 1989.

McDowell, Josh, and Wilson, Bill. *A Ready Defense*. San Bernardino, CA: Here's Life Publishers, Inc., 1990.

McDowell, Josh, and Wilson, Bill. *He Walked Among Us*. Nashville, TN: Thomas Nelson, Inc., 1993.

Reader's Digest. *ABCs of the Bible*. Pleasantville, NY: 1991.

Reader's Digest. *Who's Who in the Bible*. Pleasantville, NY: 1994.

Rosen, Moishe. *Y'shua*. Chicago, IL: Moody Bible Institute, 1982.

Ross, Hugh, Ph.D. *The Fingerprint of God*. Orange, CA: Promise Publishing Co., 1989.

Shanks, Hershel (editor). *Understanding the Dead Sea Scrolls*. New York, NY: Vintage Books, 1993.

Smith, F. LaGard. *The Daily Bible in Chronological Order*. Eugene, OR: Harvest House, 1984.

Walvoord, John F. *The Prophecy Knowledge Handbook*. Wheaton, IL: Victor Books, 1984.